For The Kophs Family

FARLEY'S

FIVE-AND-DIME

A Dime Store Novel

Renee Riva

By Renee Riva

StoneHouse Ink
2010
StoneHouse Ink
Nampa ID 83686
www.thestonepublishinghouse.com

First Hardcover Edition: 2010
First Paperback Edition: 2010
First E-Book Edition 2010

Cover design: istockphoto

Farley's Five and Dime: a novel/ by Renee Riva. -1st. ed.p.cm.
ISBN 978-0-9826078-7-9 (Paperback)

STONEHOUSE INK

Farley's Five-And-Dime

I dedicate this book to the Stardust Twins

With heartfelt thanks to those who have inspired and cheered this project along, helping to bring Mazie May Farley to life. Best friends Mazie and Maybeline were inspired by a rare and wonderful childhood friendship shared with my best buddy, Dorie Ewing. We will always be The Stardust Twins forever and ever. Here's to you li'l twin o' mine!

And to Chuck Woller, Project Manager, surfer, songwriter, editor, and friend of The Stardust Twins. Ain't No Mountain High Enough!

TABLE OF CONTENTS

Dime-Store Memoir

DIME-STORE MEMOIR

When I was a kid we owned a store...

There was nothing real special 'bout Farley's Five-and-Dime—except that I was a Farley. That, and my family lived up above the store in a small apartment we called The Loft. And my daddy built a secret slide beside the back staircase that went from The Loft right down into the store—which came in quite handy when my brother, Sammy, and me were in need of a midnight snack. Being his little sister, he always let me go first.

Our two-story slide was the talk of the town in Hog Eye Holler. And Farley's Five-and-Dime ranked right up there along with it. Hardly an hour went by that we didn't have little noses pressed up against our Front windows, checking out the latest display of toys and dolls. I, Mazie May Farley, was the one in charge of the window displays. From the time I could walk, I spent nearly every waking hour in that store, helping to make our way as a family. That's why Daddy built the slide that landed us right inside the store, so we would look forward to going to work every morning.

It was just me and Daddy and Sammy that made up our family after Mama went to heaven in 1956. I was only nine years old when she left us. I remember thinking she must have been needed pretty bad up there, 'cause I sure needed her down here, but heaven got her anyway.

The three of us ran the store without any outside help. Summers were my favorite time of all and got a little crazy at times—but a good kind of crazy—'cause when it got real busy, I got to work the soda fountain counter. The best part about that was getting to know everybody's business, and believe me, there was a lot of business to know in Hog Eye Holler.

The reason behind the big summer rush was that our store was right smack across the street from the swimming beach on Lavender Lake. Most folks don't believe us when we tell them we lived by a lake that turned lavender, but if they were ever to sit on that beach any morning when the sun was coming up over the mountains, they would swear on their life that the lake was lavender. And at night, when the sun set back down, that lake turned anywhere from hot pink to bright orange. No fooling.

All summer long the summer crowd beat a path from the beach over to the Five-and-Dime. They raided our freezers for popsicles and ice cream bars, then swung by my counter for soda fountain drinks. I knew the names of everyone who lived on that lake, as well as all the townsfolk who spent the better part of their summers at the community swimming beach. We were a pretty tight bunch that made up Hog Eye Holler.

The second I got off work, I headed straight for the beach myself. I just couldn't get enough of that sunshine. Mama once told me my freckles were kisses from the sun. But I know they really came from her, along with my strawberry red hair. I used to wear it long when Mama was here to brush it out for me, but after she died it just got so tangled, I cut it all off in a pixie cut for easy keeping.

Like I said, summers were my favorite time of year, but there was one winter that outshined all of those summers combined. I call it my "Blue Moon Winter" 'cause something happened that winter that surprised the socks off even me. And it all happened right under a full blue moon. That was years ago, but every now and again, when I look up and see that old moon shining bright in the dead of winter, I feel like I'm eleven years old again, peeking out from behind the card rack where I hid every time that crazy lady came into our store…

1

Hog Eye Holler, Kentucky

1958

"Miss Mazie, go on and fetch Mrs. Sable two cans of Christmas tree flock, if you would, please."

I slowly inch my way out from behind the card rack. "Yes, sir." That's what I call him—"sir." Daddy calls me "Miss Mazie" when I'm working, just like I'm one of the grown ups 'stead of just a kid. But only when I'm working. Otherwise, it's just "Mazie" and "Daddy." Unless he's upset with me for some reason, then it's "Mazie May", said with his eye brows pushed together.

I'm making my way back to the Christmas aisle to fetch those two cans of flock, when who should come through that front door but Billy Ray Baxter. Billy Baxter is what most folks call him. Only his own mama can call him Billy Ray and get away with it—

well, and maybe Emma Jean Jacobs. But that Billy Baxter, he's just the handsomest hunk-a-hunk you've ever laid eyes on in all of Hog Eye Holler. And me, well, I'm just Billy Baxter's best friend's little kid sister, Mazie May Farley.

So here comes Billy Ray right toward where we keep the tree flock up by the front display window. I can't even look at him without blushing like an idiot. Quick as I can, I climb up into the display window to hide b'fore he spots me. There's a big fake Christmas tree with all kinds of toys and pretty wrapped boxes underneath, and a lady mannequin wearing a red sequin dress standing next to it all. Billy's about to walk right past the window display, so I grab the closest thing to me—which happens to be a fishing pole—then I freeze like I am one of the mannequins in the little family Christmas scene.

So here I am holding a fishing pole when Billy Ray walks by. He goes to the counter right across from me and starts looking at necklaces, most likely for Emma Jean. I'm thinking I'm gonna be here all day if he doesn't hurry and pick something out. And wouldn't ya know it, right out in front of our store, tootling along the sidewalk is a bunch of boys from my school—including Jesse Deere, who loves to tease me every chance he gets. Jesse says I have a Pippi Longstocking head on a parakeet body. That's 'cause of my strawberry hair, a smile that looks like a mouth full of Chiclets, and my featherweight body on a pair o' little bird legs. But these legs can outrun just about anyone in town, including Jesse Deere.

Just as the boys pass by, I suck in my breath and hold still as a statue. At first, it looks like no one is gonna notice me... 'til Jesse takes a double take and stops dead in his tracks. He starts pointing and laughing at me like there is no tomorrow. Then all his friends join in. Behind them, a lady and her two little kids look at me like they've never seen a girl with a fishing pole before. Finally, everyone moves on—except for Billy Ray. He's still mulling over necklaces at the jewelry counter.

He suddenly walks right over, looks up at me, and says, "Hey there, Mazie," like this is just the normalist thing for me to be standing up here like this holding a fishin' pole.

"Hey, yourself, Billy," I answer back, not moving a muscle.

Billy says, "Your brother 'round here somewhere?"

"Nope, Sammy's out on a delivery to Miss Myrtle Brown's place. Should be back soon."

Billy looks at me again and cocks his head to one side. "Y'all having fun in that display up there?"

I glance over at the mannequin. "Yep, I reckon we are."

"Okay, then," he says, and strolls on back to the jewelry counter. He turns back around, "You know, Mazie, you look pretty natural up there in that display. Maybe you'll help sell some fishing poles today."

The next thing I see is Daddy heading down the aisle looking for me.

"Mazie May—what in the Sam Hill are you doing standing in that window display when you're supposed to be fetching Mrs. Sable some tree flock?" Daddy is not looking pleased.

I turn about as red as a too ripe tomato in summer. "W-well...," I begin to stammer.

"Mr. Farley," Billy cuts in, "I was just eyeing that fishin' pole up there, thinking it might be a real nice gift to give my brother for Christmas."

Daddy looks from me to Billy, then back to me again. "Well, Miss Mazie, can I count on you to get that flock—oh, never mind, I'll get it myself. You just hand Billy that pole and get yourself down from there."

"Yes, sir." When Daddy turns away I look over at Billy and mouth *thank you*. He looks right back at me and winks—*winks! At me!* I'm so flustered having Billy Ray Baxter wink at me, when I go to climb down from that window, I trip over one of the boxes under the Christmas tree, and the whole tree falls right on top of me, knocking over the mannequin, who loses her wig on the way down. So here I am laying in the display window under a fake Christmas tree and a bald mannequin, for all the world to see. And that's when I fell for Billy Ray Baxter.

2

Rickie's Rink

The way I see it, there are only two things standing between me and Billy Ray. Two years, age-wise, and Emma Jean Jacobs. The first one I can overcome by January 30th when I turn twelve, and will be only one year behind. The second one will take some scheming. For starters, every girl in Hog Eye, Kentucky is in love with Billy Ray Baxter and wants to be the one he asks to the Sweetheart Dance on Valentine's Day. So far, Emma Jean is the only one Billy Ray seems to notice though. That is gonna have to change by February 14th, and I intend to make sure it does. Lucky for me, Farley's Five-and-Dime soda counter is the one place I can always count on Emma Jean to come looking for Billy Ray. And that is exactly where I plan to fight this battle.

******

Friday night is our busiest night for the soda counter during the winter. Nearly every kid in Hog Eye comes by before or after roller skating for a vanilla Coke and fries. I fetch the Cokes, Sammy makes the fries. The best part is, I get to go skating in between the *before* and *after* crowds, but Sammy has to stay here to cover the stragglers. I'm waiting for Billy Ray and Emma Jean to show up in the *before* bunch, but they never come.

My best friend, Maybeline Zirkle pops her head in the front door. "You ready to go, Mazie? It's cold as all get out—better wear your snow boots." Rickie's Rink is only across the street and down the block from our store, but it's been snowing something fierce all day long. I pull my snow boots on, and grab my hat and gloves hanging by the door.

"I'll be back before the *after* crowd hits," I yell to Daddy, somewhere in the store, even though I can't see him.

"Be sure you are," he yells back from aisle three.

Me and Maybeline slip and slide our way over to Rickie's and get in line behind the other late comers. The good part about coming late is you only have to stand outside and freeze for half as long as the early comers do.

Once we're finally inside, we strip all of our snow gear off into a pile by the big pot belly stove. That's where we leave all of our wet stuff to dry while we're skating. There's nothing better than putting on a warmed up pair of mitts for the cold trek back home. After we clothespin our gloves and hats to a string hanging above the stove, we head to the counter to grab our skates. I used to hope for the newest skates but they always hurt my feet, so now I'm happy just to get any old worn in pair.

Me and Maybeline are lacing up when I suddenly spy *her* out on the floor—with her long dark curls flowing along behind her. *"She's here!"*

Maybeline looks at me like I'm nutty. "Who's here?"

"Her."

"Her, who?"

"Her, Emma Jean."

Maybeline looks like that means absolutely nothing to her.

"Okay, I'll tell you. But you have to swear, cross your heart, hope to die, you will never tell another soul as long as you live. *Swear?"*

"Swear."

I pull Maybeline back over to a corner by the stove. "Okay, you know Billy Ray Baxter?"

Maybeline rolls her eyes. "Who doesn't know Billy Ray Baxter?"

"Well, the other day I was hiding up in the Christmas display when Billy Ray came by. He asked if I was having fun up there, and I told him yes, I was. So Billy says I looked kinda natural up there. Then my daddy comes by and is about to give me the what for, cause I didn't get Mrs. Sable's tree flock, right?"

"Right..."

"Well, Billy Ray tells Daddy he's thinking about getting that fishing pole that I was holding up there in that Christmas display. So Daddy never gives me the what for. And the next thing I know, Billy... Billy Ray Baxter... *winks at me.*"

"He didn't!"

"Did so. Right there in the display window."

"Wow." Maybeline shakes her head. "But... what's that got to do with Emma Jean?"

"Maybeline—everybody knows that Billy Ray is sweet on Emma Jean."

"Yeah, so?"

"So, Emma Jean is my competition now. I have to get Billy to dump her in time to ask me to the Sweetheart Dance."

Maybeline's eyes pop nearly clear out of her head. "Mazie May Farley, if you think you're going to get Billy Ray Baxter to ask you to that dance, you need to have your head examined. You're eleven years-old and he's *thirteen!* Stop talking nonsense and let's go skate before you have to be back at the soda counter."

"I think he might just be waiting for me to turn twelve. How else do you explain Billy Ray covering for me in front of my daddy and winking at me?"

"He's probably just being nice to you for being Sammy's kid sister."

As me and Maybeline start to make our way into the rink, they call out the Hokey Pokey over the speakers. "C'mon." I grab Maybeline and pull her with me into the circle, right straight across from Emma Jean so I can keep an eye on her.

We do the Hokey Pokey and we turn ourselves around, just like the song goes, but the whole time I've got one eye on Emma Jean and the other on Billy Ray.

"And just how do you plan to get Billy away from *her?*" Maybeline suddenly wants to know.

"Watch me."

As soon as the Hokey Pokey ends they call "pairs only" on the speakers. Billy Ray skates up to

Emma Jean and off they go around the rink holding hands.

"C'mon!" I grab Maybeline's hand and pull her out on the rink.

"W-ait! I want to see if a boy asks me to skate before I settle for going with you."

"Maybeline, the only boy in Hog Eye Holler that would ask you to skate is my brother, and he's not here tonight, so c'mon!"

Maybeline takes my hand and we start around the rink. The more I'm watching Billy Ray and Emma Jean, the more I'm burning up inside.

"Time to execute my plan."

"What have you got up your sleeve, Mazie?"

"If Billy Ray were to suddenly realize that Emma Jean Jacobs is a big klutz on wheels, he might just dump her for someone who can skate half way decent—like *me*."

"That's crazy, Mazie!"

I just ignore Maybeline and begin to slow way down, waiting for the honeymooners to catch up to me.

Maybeline pulls her hand away from mine and skates away shaking her head.

I move over by the railing and just wait for that Emma Jean to skate by me. Just when she and Billy Ray are about to pass by, I stick the toe of my skate out right in front of Emma Jean.

Emma Jean shrieks as her skates collide with mine, but instead of falling flat on her face like I'd planned, she plows right into me and sends me spinning out of control. I go flying into the center of the rink where I wobble back and forth like a piece of Jell-O on a spoon, then land flat on my fanny. Everyone's staring at me. Jesse Deere is howling his fool head off, and Emma Jean falls right into Billy Ray's arms. He's so wrapped up in making sure he catches her, he doesn't even glance in my direction to see if I live or die. I drag my sorry little behind out of the rink and untie my skates.

"Smooth move," Jesse snickers, as he skates past me.

"Oh, go skate yourself into a wall," I yell after him. Now I'm fuming at both Emma Jean *and* Jesse Deere. No matter. I still have exactly one month, three weeks, and six days to snag my catch.

3

Love Bugs

One week before Christmas, Billy Ray comes back into the Five-and-Dime and buys that necklace he was looking at. I'm sweeping the aisle, dreaming about what it will feel like when he buys a necklace for me come next Christmas. A brilliant idea suddenly pops into my head.

"Hey, Billy, would you like me to gift wrap that for you?"

"Sure, Mazie, that would be swell."

"Okay, I'll just take it in the back where we keep our wrapping paper and fix it up real nice for you."

Billy Ray hands off the necklace. Slipping into the back room, I toss it on the counter beside all the ribbon and bows. *Hmmm, let's see, black would be a nice color for Emma Jean—the official color of goodbye and good riddance.* Smiling to myself, I cut the paper to fit the box. Just before wrapping it up, I scan the room for something special to add to it. *Ah, dead bugs in the window sill.* I saunter over for a closer look. *These should add a nice touch.* I pick out a few choice flies and a bright green beetle, and sprinkle them right inside the gift box on top of the necklace. *Merry Christmas, Emma Jean, the Dead Bug Queen.* Between the bugs and the black gift wrap she'll probably never speak to Billy Ray again. I top the whole thing off with a nice red bow just to throw Billy Ray off enough to still give it to her.

When I come out of the back room with the gift, Billy Ray's smile begins to fade. *"Black?"*

"Oh, black is really *in* this Christmas. It's the latest thing in romance—black with a red bow. Funny, huh?"

"Yeah, funny." His smile comes back. "Thanks, Mazie. I'll bet one day a young man will be giving you something like this for Christmas."

You got that right, buster. And it will be you. Minus the bugs.

******

Sunday morning, I'm sitting in Sunday school at Holy Cross listening to Miss Tiffany talk about loving our neighbor during the Christmas season by doing kind deeds for them.

Good thing Emma Jean is not my neighbor.

"And who is our neighbor?" Miss Tiffany asks.

I'm thinking of old Mr. Martin, and how just maybe I'll bake him up a sugar loaf for Christmas.

"Our neighbor is anyone God brings along our path, and whether we like them or not, we are to show love to them."

Oh, great. Not what I wanted to hear.

"This is the time to make things right. Right the wrongs of the past year, so we can spend Christmas with a joyful heart and a clear conscience."

Can we just settle for the joyful heart? I realize I have only two more days 'til Christmas before Emma Jean opens that gift box and I ruin Christmas for two people.

I toss and turn all night with those words ringing in my ears; *"Right the wrong. Right the wrong."*

"Okay, already!" I say out loud. *"I will.* Tomorrow."

******

First thing Christmas Eve morning, I find myself on Emma Jean's front porch. It takes me ten minutes to finally ring the bell. Mrs. Jacobs comes to the door and calls Emma Jean downstairs.

"Mazie—what a surprise," Emma Jean says, with that sweet Southern belle twang of hers. If she weren't so sincere it would be sickening.

"Hi Emma Jean. Merry Christmas." I hand her a sugar loaf with a green bow on top. I even put green dye in the batter to make it match the bow.

"Why, Mazie, that is so thoughtful of you. Would you like to come in?"

"Umm, maybe just for a minute." We go into their front room and sit by their big fake white Christmas tree. I always wanted a fake white tree. They look so… clean.

32

"Are you all done shopping for Christmas?" she asks me.

"All done. It's pretty easy to shop when you live above a store."

"Oh, yeah," Emma Jean giggles. "I forgot."

"Emma Jean, there's... there's something I need to tell you." *Lord... do I have to?* "Umm, it's just that... you know that gift that Billy Ray is giving you for Christmas..."

Emma Jean tilts her head, waiting for me to spit it out.

"Well, I need to tell you... about that black wrapping paper..."

"Wasn't that just the sweetest color combo?" Emma Jean blurts out. "I told Billy Ray there is something so romantic about black and red together. Don't you think so, too?"

"Uh... y-eah. I told Billy the same thing." *Drat! She liked it.* "But when you open it tomorrow..."

"Oh, I already did! Billy Ray couldn't wait for me to see what he got me, so I opened it last night. I couldn't believe my eyes when I took the lid off. How on earth did he know?"

"Know what?"

"That I have a fetish for bugs! I have an incredible bug collection, and I've looked the longest time for a June bug, and could never find one in such perfect condition. When I went to open the box, there on top of my beautiful necklace was the very bug I've been looking for—with its green metallic wings still intact! I think I love that June bug even more than the necklace." She giggles.

"No kidding?" *That figures.*

"Now here you are bringing me a sugar loaf and I feel just awful for not having a gift for you."

"Ah, it's nothing, really." *I probably could've brought a lump of coal and you'd love that too.*

"Now, what was it you wanted to tell me?"

"Uh, just that… you have a Merry Christmas, Emma Jean."

"Same to you Mazie Farley, and thanks for stopping by."

4

Best Buds

The next stop on the list is Maybeline's house. In between Emma Jean's and Maybeline's, a blizzard strikes up and I can hardly even see ten feet in front of myself. By the time I reach the Zirkle's I look like an abominable snowman. I tromp up the front steps and bang on the door. I'm half frozen to death by the time Mrs. Zirkle answers the door.

"Land sakes, Mazie—what are you doing out in this weather?"

"Merry Christmas, Mrs. Zirkle," I chatter back, through my icicle teeth. "I wanted to drop a present by for Maybeline."

"Hey, Mazie!" Maybeline calls from the family room. "C'mon back here!"

Mrs. Zirkle all but yanks me in out of the cold. "How 'bout if you go in and warm up by the fire, Mazie, while I make y'all some hot chocolate?"

"Yes, ma'am," I answer back, thinking how nice it must be to have a mama to make hot chocolate for you whenever you're cold. I pull off my snow boots, shedding a pile of fresh snow in the foyer while I'm at it, and head for the fire.

Maybeline's sitting on the hearth by the fire, holding a big box all wrapped up in shiny gold paper with a silver bow.

"Who's *that* for?"

"My best friend."

I feel a twinge of jealousy rising up. "Which one?"

"*You* of course, silly Mazie!"

I was hoping she'd say that.

Mrs. Zirkle comes in with two big mugs of hot chocolate piled sky high with whipped cream. While we're sippin' away, I tell Maybeline all about the black paper and bug-lovin' Emma Jean.

"Boy, Mazie, you sure got off the hook easy for doing something so stupid."

"Yeah, well, you don't have to put it quite like that." Maybeline is a say-it- like-it-is kind of person.

She shrugs. "Hey, what are friends for?"

"They're for giving presents to." I toss a tiny package to Maybeline. "You go first."

Maybeline carefully takes the plaid ribbon off of my gift box and opens it very slowly. "No bugs, right?"

"No bugs."

Inside is a small gold heart-shaped locket with a tiny picture of me on one side and a tiny picture of Maybeline on the other. Maybeline gasps. "It's the friendship locket from your store… the one I wanted."

"It's a *best friends'* locket." I help her put it on. I know she likes it 'cause she's only told me a hundred times that that's what she wanted for Christmas.

Maybeline holds the locket up and smiles. "Thanks, Mazie. Now open yours!" She hands me the big gold box. I just rip right into it. No point in wasting time on paper you're just going to throw away anyway. When I lift the lid I'm looking at a great big scrapbook with a picture of me and Maybeline on the front. We're sitting on stools at our soda counter, sharing a giant root beer float with two straws.

"It's filled with all of the pictures we took of us over the whole year, Mazie!"

"You made this? This musta taken you all year to make."

."Yep." Maybeline is looking mighty proud of herself. "And there's room to add more pictures too."

"I don't have any scrapbooks, only a small photo album of me with... my... mama..."

"Oh, Mazie, I didn't mean for it to make you sad."

"It doesn't make me sad that you gave me this, Maybeline. I love the scrapbook. I'm just sad because it's Christmas... and the more Christmas's that go by without her... well, sometimes... she doesn't feel as real anymore."

Maybeline nods.

"Seems when you can't she your mama everyday, you just start to forget... what she looked like."

"I bet your mama was real pretty," Maybeline says.

We just sit in front of the fire for a long time, watching the flames, looking at pictures, and being best friends.

5

Humbug

On Christmas Eve, Daddy, Sammy, and I are finishing up at the Five-and-Dime with last minute Christmas shoppers. Some people really cut it close on buying their presents! And they are in such a frenzy to pack it all in before we close that they tear through the aisles like tornados on wheels! By the time the last of 'em clear out, we are left with a big fat mess to deal with. My stomach starts to growl just looking at it all. We could be here all night.

Daddy takes one look around and announces, "Let's just shut it down and go enjoy Christmas! We'll save it all for Santa's elves."

Daddy's been working hard all of December and only gets Sundays and Christmas Day off. We lock up shop in two shakes and head down the block to our favorite restaurant *Country Vittles.*

We love, love, *love* having someone else cook for us. *Country Vittles* is a big old log cabin with a stuffed moose head on the wall, and Christmas lights dangling off the antlers. A roaring fire blazes away in the river stone fireplace, old mining lanterns light up the tables, and the smell of fried chicken and dumplin's is in the air.

We always sit close to the fire, and order three plates of the special, no matter what it is. It's always good and we like to be surprised at what they bring us. It's either meatloaf and mashed potatoes, corned beef and hash, or chicken and dumplin's. We all guess it's gonna be the chicken and dumplin's 'cause that's what the whole place smells like.

Nellie is our favorite waitress of all, so we grab the big corner booth in her section. Nellie lives with her Grandparents and her Aunt Velma, who are the owners of *Country Vittles.* We have had the misfortune of getting old Velma one time too many as our waitress, so we avoid being seated in her section like the plague. She is the grumpiest waitress in all of Kentucky, and Daddy refuses to pay good money to put up with an attitude like hers. But our Nellie is pretty as all get out, and has a blonde pony tail that swings back 'n forth when she walks.

She clip-clops over to our table in her high heel cowgirl boots, which I just love the sound of. They're light pink with fringe down the sides. The clippy-clop sound reminds me of ponies prancing down Lavender Lane in the Fourth of July parade. I want to get me some of those boots one day so I can clip-clop around the aisles of the Five-and-Dime. Daddy says I'm too young for heels like that just yet.

"Hello, li'l darlin's!" Nellie hands us each a menu, even though we never use them. "Y'all hungry, or you just come here to see me?"

"Both," I tell her.

"Well, then, let's feed ya!"

"Three specials, please," Daddy says, and hands back all the menus.

"You got it," she says, and swings her way back toward the kitchen in her fine country skirt, keeping in step to the country music playing. She even do-si-do's the bus boy, like she's in the middle of a square dance. She swings her way through the swinging kitchen doors, and two seconds later, she comes swinging her way back to our table with some hot biscuits 'n butter. I watch her every move when I'm here 'cause I want to grow up to be just like her. I already practice my pony tail swing when I'm working the counter at the Five-and-Dime. My hair is just now finally long enough to wear in a super short ponytail. No more pixie-cuts for this cowgirl or I will never look like Nellie.

When our plates show up, Daddy blesses our food and thanks The Lord for sending us Jesus for Christmas. We dig right in and no one says another word, except "mmm-mmm" through the whole meal. We are just enjoying our home cooked country meal, and for once, having no body asking us for more ketchup or anything.

Once we're full up, we try and remember what we had for last year's Christmas special and decided it was the same thing. While we're chatting away about past Christmas dinners, Nellie surprises us with a complimentary Flaming Christmas Cherries Jubilee. She sets the torched cherries right down in front of me. I'm trying to dodge the flames, wondering how I'm supposed to eat something that's on fire.

I quickly get the picture that we don't have to eat the flames, but flames or no flames, I'm so stuffed from dinner I barely have room for anything more. Somehow we all manage to grunt and groan our way through it just to be polite. Just when we're all about to burst, Daddy asks for the bill.

While Nellie's busy adding up our total on her little tablet, Daddy asks her where she'll be spending Christmas.

"Right here," she says. "This is all the family I have anymore. My Grandma and Grandpa are gonna need some help serving up Christmas dinner to *Nana's Knitters.*"

"What's Nana's Knitters?" I ask.

"It's a knitting club my Grandma started for elderly women in the community years ago. Many of them are widowed and have no family in the area to spend the holidays with so Grandma puts on a special Christmas dinner for them every year." Nellie leans down closer and whispers, "You're welcome to stop by and meet them Miss Mazie— they're some of the sweetest l'il gals you could ever hope to meet."

I remember Miss Mabel Brown talking about some knitting club she belonged to. I'd almost bet it's the same one.

Nellie hands Daddy the dinner check. "We get a pretty good turnout every year," she says. "Lots of nice folks."

Daddy looks up at Nellie and nods. He opens his wallet and without even counting, hands her a couple of big bills. "Merry Christmas, Nellie." he says to her. "Keep the change."

******

We walk home by way of the park tonight to see the living nativity that the town of Hog Eye puts on every Christmas Eve. The newest baby boy, born closest to Christmas Eve, gets to play Baby Jesus every year. This has caused some competition between some of the expectant mothers in the past as they have all tried to plan their baby's birth around Christmastime. One year, two baby boys came along on the same day, but we couldn't have two Baby Jesus's, so they had to take turns and work in shifts. It's quite an honor to be Baby Jesus in this town. You get your picture in the newspaper and go down in the Hog Eye Holler Hall of Fame. There's a whole wall in the Hog Eye Holler Museum of all the Baby Jesus's from way back. Some of the first Baby Jesus's are older than the hills by now. For some folks in this town, that is their only claim to fame.

Just when we're walking by the shepherds, one of them tries to trip me with his staff.

"Jesse Deere, I know that's you inside of that dumb shepherd costume. You couldn't fool me if you tried. Besides, you wore that same dumb costume last year."

"I'll play Joseph next year, Mazie, if you'll play Mary."

"I think you'd make a better donkey."

"I'll be the front half, if you'll be the back."

"Go herd some sheep, Jesse."

"Merry Christmas to you too, Mazie." He laughs.

Right then, Billy Ray comes running up and whacks Sammy on the back. "Hey Farley—it's about time you got outta that Five-and-Dime for a change."

"Hey, Billy—it's about time I see you without Emma Jean for a change."

Ditto for me. Now's my chance to make an impression without *her* hanging around.

Billy Ray looks over at me. "Hey, Mazie, thanks for sneaking Emma Jean's favorite bug inside that gift for me—she loved it! How'd you know she wanted that?"

"Mmm, just a lucky guess." *Just bad luck.*

"I think your bug really helped to win her heart for me."

Doesn't THAT just make me feel all warm inside. "Glad to help," I lie.

******

Daddy says he's heading on home and will see us all later. The three of us wander around, looking at all of the animals in the manger. While I'm racking my brains for something clever to say, Billy Ray and Sammy wander off together, leaving me just standing here by myself next to a goat who's looking at me like we're in some kinda stare-down. I'm thinking there may not have been a goat at the birth of Jesus. "What are you looking at?" I say. I'd rather be staring at Billy Ray than a Billy goat. "I don't remember seeing anything that looks like you in any manger scenes." Rather than standing here talking to a goat, I decide I may as well walk on home.

Making my way down Lavender Lane, it starts to snow. I love the smell of snow. It smells so... clean. Everything around me is dark and quiet, except the crunch of my snow boots. I'm walking along, looking at all the bright Christmas lights on the rooftops, and peeking through all the windows as I pass by. It's fun to see all of the different Christmas trees and check how many presents are under each one. I start to wonder if next Christmas Billy Ray will be walking me home.

"Hey, Mazie," a voice calls out from behind me.

Billy Ray? I spin around faster than a ballerina in a music box only to find dumb Jesse Deere—still in his costume. "Oh... it's you."

"Mind if I walk home with you?"

"Do I have a choice?"

"Not really. I'm afraid of being alone in the dark."

"Right."

So here I am walking home in the snow with someone dressed up like a shepherd, instead of with Billy Ray Baxter. This is not exactly the vision of romance I had in my mind a few minutes ago.

When we finally reach my store, Jesse says, "Well, night Mazie." He shoves something in my hand. "Merry Christmas!" Then he takes off running down the block.

Standing under the street light, I look down at the package all wrapped up in duct tape. It takes forever to wrestle off the tape, but I finally rip it off and find a small, round, tin box inside. I slowly lift the lid and a huge Slinky snake springs out at me. "Auugghh!" I scream, and throw the whole thing up in the air. *That darn Jesse Deere!* I know he heard me scream. I can hear him laughing all the way down the block.

So, Emma Jean is getting a beautiful jewel necklace for Christmas from the most wonderful boy in school, and I, Mazie May, get a Slinky snake from dumb Jesse Deere in a shepherd's costume. I'm beginning to understand how Scrooge felt during the holidays. Bah, humbug.

6

A House Full of Christmas

Christmas morning is snowing and blowing like crazy, but lucky for us, our steam radiator is frantically hissing away as well. It doesn't take much to keep our little loft warm and toasty. And we have a dwarf noble fur tree in our front room, all trimmed with lights and a star. The rest of our ornaments ended up down on the tree in the window display in the store, 'cause we had more ornaments than we had a tree for up here. Under our little tree are ten presents total, averaging 'bout three a piece, 'cept for Sammy who got four, thanks to Maybeline, who has had a crush on my brother her whole life. I keep telling her that he only likes her as his kid sister's best friend, but that's as far as it goes. It's hard to convince a girl in love that they've got their head too far in the clouds to see the truth of the matter when it comes to boys.

Sammy and I are listening to Nat King Cole's Christmas music while we wait for Daddy's morning coffee to reach his brainwaves. He needs to wake up enough to watch us pick out our presents. I say "pick out," on account of that's what we get to do every Christmas morning. Daddy lets us slide down into the store and pick out one thing—anything we want—for our Christmas present from him. It's usually something we've had our eye all year, but sometimes it takes so long for Christmas to come that we get tired of what we first wanted and switch to something else.

Me and Sammy are waiting at the top of the slide for the green light from Daddy.

"Okay," Daddy yells from the kitchen, "head on down!"

When we were little, we always went down the slide head first, but now that we're older we just go feet first.

I already know just what I want, but I like to wander through the aisles real slow just to make sure I don't want to change my mind at the last minute. Sammy heads straight for the camping aisle. He's had his eye on a Swiss army knife that he's planning to take on his trek to Canada this summer. Sammy is pretty matter-of-fact when it comes to picking out what he wants.

After I've wandered my way through every aisle, I swing over to the rock polisher I've had my sights on for a good long time and scoop it up with both arms. I have wanted a rock polisher for three years now, but I had to get over my Barbie Doll fetish first. I just traded my entire collection this fall at the Shop-n-Swap for a pair of ice skates. I guess that means I'm over Barbie now.

Daddy follows behind us, smiling to himself as we hike back upstairs with our presents. Sammy disappears to his room and returns with our joint gift for Daddy. It's the same thing every year—a new selection of flannel shirts from The Sears and Roebuck catalog—the double thick kind that he wears every single day of winter. Now he can retire *the old ones we* gave him last year. Sammy and I swap each other three matinee tickets that we bought for each other, and call it good. Then I haul out my bucket of a bazillion rocks that I've been collecting along the shores of Lavender Lake for my entire life, and begin to sort them out in order of which ones will get to take the first tumble in the rock tumbler.

******

"Make way for the ham!" Uncle Tooty yells, coming through the front door, carrying a huge Christmas ham in a crate. Aunt Birdie is close behind with the scalloped potatoes, relish tray, rolls, and pies, all in a big cardboard box, followed by Grandma Blossom with all the presents. And Banjo, their short-legged corgi, is bringing up the rear, sporting a big red bow.

Grandma Blossom's real name is Grandma Rose, but when I was little I forgot which flower she was named after so I called her Grandma Blossom, and somehow it stuck for good. The Farley bunch loves to come to Hog Eye for the holidays 'cause we get a lotta snow up here in the holler and they don't get so much down in the valley. Grandma Blossom and Aunt Birdie cook up a storm for about a week before they come, then they pack it all up, load it into the Woody, and drive on up here. They throw in their down comforters and pillows just in case. If it's still snowing by the time we've all stuffed ourselves silly, they just all sleep on the floor around the Christmas tree, and wait for morning to brave the drive back home. I always pray they get snowed in for the night 'cause it makes Christmas last longer that way. Besides that, I get to sleep under the Christmas tree with Banjo. That's as close as I've ever come to having a dog of my own.

Uncle Tooty is Daddy's big brother. They like to get going on their fishing stories together with Sammy, and see who can brag about catching the biggest fish since the last time they bragged about it. Uncle Tooty is a little *different* when it comes to fishing. He actually likes to sneak off in the pitch dark to go fishing in the middle of the night. He calls it Moon Fishing. Says he feels part of nature that way—out there under the moon and stars and all. The funny thing is, he hardly ever catches anything at night. I once asked Uncle Tooty how he could expect to catch fish when they're all asleep and it's too dark for them to even see the worm on his hook even if they did open their eyes. He said, "You know, Mazie, for some men, it's really more about spending some peaceful time in the outdoors than it is about catching fish."

"Well, now that I know that," Aunt Birdie says, "I won't feel so bad tellin' you to just stay home next time and take the garbage outside if you're really just wantin' a good outdoors experience."

Uncle Tooty looks at me. "That's why men just say they're goin' fishin'."

******

While the guys are busy talking fish, me and "the girls," as Grandma Blossom calls us, put out all of the Christmas dinner fixin's and talk about way more interesting things than slimy fish. Aunt Birdie asks me what I want for my birthday next month. "Waltzing lessons," I tell her, so I will know how to waltz at the Sweetheart Dance.

They have ballroom dance lessons at the grange every Friday night for kids over ten years old. I figure I could get in at least two lessons before Valentine's Day if I got them for my birthday. I would've asked for them for Christmas if I'd been thinking. That way I'd be an experienced dancer by the time the Sweetheart dance rolls around. But two lessons are better than none.

We used to go see Mama's family on Christmas, but since Mama passed away right at Christmastime, her family still has a hard time celebrating anything that reminds them of losing her. It was springtime when Mama first got sick, but she didn't pass away until Christmastime. Her mama, Grandma Ellie, says I look just like my mama did when she was little, which makes Grandma Ellie terribly sad, so I don't get to see my Grandma Ellie very often. Maybe one day I won't make her too sad to see me. For now, that's just the way it is.

*****

Once the food is all spread out on the table, Uncle Tooty carves up the Christmas ham, then we give thanks to God and ask a blessing on our meal and family. Aunt Birdie's orange-cranberry rolls are a big hit. I make sure to fill up on those first before I'm too full from ham and potatoes.

While we're all busy enjoying the feast, we get to hear all the latest news and gossip from down in the valley. Uncle Tooty gives us the news—Aunt Birdie gives us the gossip. She sure knows how to tell a story or two. Aunt Birdie tells it better than *Storytime Theater* on the radio. She pulls the relish tray over to snack on while she tells us each juicy morsel. "The latest scandal," she says, while chomping on a carrot, "is over the McDougal's daughter, Fanny Fay, who ran off to elope with J.D. Farkle. Now mind you, these two families have been feuding it out like the Hatfield's and the McCoy's for years, ever since

The Farkle family caught Mr. and Mrs. McDougal sipping moonshine at the Methodist's church picnic, and nicknamed them Sipsy and Tipsy McDougal— names which have followed them to this day. And now they're all forced to be in-laws with one another. I get a chuckle out of it myself, but I have a notion that Sipsy McDougal is just sick over the fact that her daughter's name is now Fanny Fay Farkle. The town folks are already joking about them naming their babies; Freddie, Frieda, and Frank Farkle. Try saying that real fast while munching on a carrot."

I love Aunt Birdie's laugh—she doesn't really laugh, she chortles. Aunt Birdie pauses just long enough to poke her finger into an olive and plop it in her mouth, then continues. "That's not half as bad as the Steins naming their baby boy Frank Nathan. Think of that poor kid going through life as Frank N. Stein."

Frank N. Stein… Frank N. Stein… Frankenstein! I finally get it.

Some things Aunt Birdie tells us aren't really so funny, but she always makes me laugh just by the way she tells it.

Once Aunt Birdie runs out of stories, I hint that the presents under the tree sure are wrapped nicely. "Oh for Pete's sake!" Aunt Birdie yells, "The presents—I nearly forgot!"

We all make our way over to the Christmas tree, with me and Banjo leading the way. Uncle Tooty plays Santa, as usual, and hands out all of the gifts. I can pretty well guess that whatever I'm getting was knitted by Grandma Blossom and Aunt Birdie. They are the only reason I have not frozen to death up here in the holler over the past eleven years.

"Oh, it's just what I wanted… a pink scarf, a hat, and matching mittens!" I have a dozen sets just like them, but it's nice to get a new set each year. Daddy and Sammy get their traditional knit stockings—which they will wear holes in by next Christmas. I wasn't very creative this year and just picked out some nice bubble bath for the women, and stinky tobacco for Uncle Tooty's pipe. I'm hoping to make everyone rock jewelry by next Christmas.

After trying on my new pink scarf ensemble, I park myself in front of the television for the Christmas Day specials.

Sure enough, just as I'd hoped, half way through "The Bells of St. Mary" the snow starts coming down hard. Everyone breaks long enough to grab a big piece of sweet potato pie, then out come all of the pillows and down comforters. We throw all the bedding in front of the television set and settle back in for the rest of the movie. Our front room quickly becomes wall to wall blankets, pillows, pie, and people. Oh, and a puppy—on my pillow. When I look around The Loft at all of these people eating, laughing, and carrying on, I just tingle all over. There's nothing better than a house full of Christmas.

7

Please Pass the Maple Syrup

Uncle Tooty wakes us all up at the crack of dawn and says he wants to take us all out to breakfast. Aunt Birdie tells him he's out of his tree and makes him leave us alone 'til she's good and ready to get up. By the time that happens, it's nearly noon and time for lunch instead of breakfast.

Uncle Tooty loves to go to *Country Vittles* every time he visits. And every time we go, he does something that makes me want to crawl under the table, or announce to the crowd that we're really not related. We just never know what Uncle Tooty is capable of doing in a crowd, but, sooner than later, we always find out.

Nellie comes swinging out to our table in a to-die-for red and white country Christmas get up—with matching boots, of course. "Yall have yourselves a nice Christmas?" she asks.

"You bet yer booty we did!" Uncle Tooty yells, real loud.

Nellie says she remembers Uncle Tooty from last time he came to visit. Who wouldn't? He put Super Gloo on all the quarters that he left for a tip and glued them down to the table top. By the time she went to gather them up, they were stuck fast. She had a heck of a time getting them all un-stuck. Says she broke nearly all of her fingernails by the time she was done. At least he left her a big tip— hopefully enough to get a manicure after all that.

Nellie pours hot coffee for all the grown ups, and starts taking orders.

"I've got a hankering for some flapjacks and maple syrup," Grandma Blossom announces.

Even though it's lunch time, my stomach is still in breakfast mode too. "Ditto on the flapjacks," I add.

By the time the rest of us have finished ordering, Uncle Tooty is still studying his menu like he's gonna be taking an exam when he's done.

Nellie looks like she knows she's in for trouble. "So, what can I get for you, Uncle Tooty?"

"Well, let's see. This here sirloin burger on a bun sounds pretty tasty. That come with fries?"

"You bet yer booty, Uncle Tooty," Nellie jokes back.

"Okay. Here's what I want. I want that sirloin burger on a bun with fries...and ketchup. Got that?"

Nellie writes it all down. "Got it."

"Now, what all comes on that burger?"

"Onion, lettuce, and mayonnaise."

"What? No pickle?"

"I'd be happy to add a pickle."

"Okay. Add the pickle please... but could you toss on some bacon while you're at it?"

Nellie jots down *pickle and bacon.*

"I'd like some cheese too," he adds.

"Cheese." She jots that down.

"Make that two slices of cheese, please. You know... A slice of tomato might be nice too."

"Two slices cheese, add tomato."

"So, what do we got now?" Uncle Tooty asks.

A big fat mess, I'm thinking.

"Um, that leaves you with a bacon, cheese, lettuce, onion, mayonnaise, pickle, and ketchup sirloin burger on a bun with fries."

"Perfect." Uncle Tooty flips shut his menu and hands it back to Nellie, then takes a big gulp of his coffee, looking like he is on top of the world. Then he suddenly says, "Hold on… Let's change that to a grilled cheese with fries."

Daddy looks at Nellie with apologetic eyes. Grandma Blossom and Aunt Birdie look at each other and roll their eyes. Sammy looks at me and tries not to laugh. And I begin to zip my parka all the way up to my nose, hoping no one in here recognizes me. Nellie just smiles, thanks us all for our orders, and trots off to the kitchen.

Uncle Tooty is our sole entertainment for the next fifteen minutes. When our order is ready, Nellie returns with a bright red kiddie's plate, sporting a grilled cheese sandwich with plastic zoo animals on top, and places it directly in front of Uncle Tooty with a smile. "Bon Appetite," she says, and clip-clops away with her ponytail swinging from side to side.

Daddy looks over at Uncle Tooty and grins. "I think Nellie got the best of you on that one, big brother."

"She's a fun little whipper snapper, ain't she?" Uncle Tooty admits.

I just love Nellie. I slather my flapjacks with whipped butter and dump on my little pitcher of warmed up maple syrup. I am so glad I picked the flapjacks—especially after looking at Uncle Tooty's plate, which, by the way, he's hasn't touched. He's staring at my plate like maybe he'd like to change his mind one more time. Once we're all set and done giving thanks, Nellie re-appears with a kiddie-sized plate of kiddie-sized flapjacks, piled high with strawberries and whipped cream. "It's on the house, Uncle Tooty," she says, plopping it in front of him, and scurries off.

I unzip my parka collar and we all dig in, including Uncle Tooty, who seems pleased as a pig in a poke. "Bon appetite," I say, and raise my fork to Uncle Tooty. From that point on the meal is blissfully quiet, as we are all too busy eating to talk—even Uncle Tooty—thank goodness.

******

The second we're finished eating, Uncle Tooty says he wants to order dessert. I slowly zip my collar back up to my nose. Wouldn't it be just my luck to have Billy Ray appear at a time like this?

8

New Year's Eve

1959

On the last day of the year, nearly the whole town of Hog Eye gathers at Patterson's Pond for the New Year's Eve ice skating festival that goes from morning 'til midnight. All of the shiny new skates and snow saucers that were discovered under Christmas trees on Christmas morning begin to appear around the pond. I'm wearing my Barbie trade-in skates for the first time. They were a tiny bit big when I first got them but they seem to fit just right now.

"Hey there, Mazie Farley!" Maybeline calls from the top of the slope, and begins sliding her way down toward the pond. "Did you hear the secret?" she yells.

"What secret?" I yell back.

She slips and slides her way across the pond in her new snow boots. "The Billy Baxter and Emma Jean secret," she yells back, so loud that the whole town can hear.

What now?

Maybeline is out of breath by the time she reaches me, but manages to spill it out in short gasps. "Everybody's saying that Billy Baxter is planning to kiss Emma Jean tonight at midnight—at the Five-and-Dime's New Year's Eve party!"

"*My* Five-and-Dime?"

"What other Five-and-Dime is there in Hog Eye Holler? You're the only place in town besides the pond that stays open 'til midnight on New Year's."

"Yeah, but not so that Billy Ray can kiss Emma Jean." Now my day is ruined and it's barely even begun. Right as I'm thinking that, I get whopped upside the head by a snow ball.

"Jesse Deere—you'll pay for that!" I take off after him as fast as my silver skates can carry me. When I finally catch up to him I push him hard as I can across the ice. He goes skidding full speed off the edge of the pond right into a snow bank. His entire face disappears into a wall of snow. "That oughta fix him for awhile."

"Geez, Mazie, you could really hurt him doing that," Maybeline warns me.

"Jesse Deere is the last person on earth I need right now in the middle of this kissing crisis."

"You're taking this kissing stuff a little too personal if ya ask me."

"Well, *it is* personal. If I'm going to the Sweetheart Dance with Billy, I don't want him kissing that Emma Jean. Somehow I have to keep their lips apart for six more weeks."

Maybeline sits on the edge of the pond to put her skates on. "Mazie, I thought you learned your lesson with the beetle fiasco. I hate to be the one to say it, but…"

I give her a glare that says she'd better not say another word.

"Never mind. C'mon, let's skate."

We're in the middle of the pond skating crazy-eights, when who should skate by holding hands but Romeo and Juliet, themselves. I grab hold of Maybeline's arm and head us over to the burn barrel where I pretend to be warming my hands. "Listen, Maybeline, I'm working the soda counter tonight at the New Year's party. I think I have the perfect solution to this whole problem…"

******

New Year's Eve at Farley's Five-and-Dime has been a tradition since the first year we opened our doors. We sell a ton of candy and popcorn to movie-goers before the show starts down the block, then everyone pours back in here afterwards for sodas and ice cream 'til midnight strikes. We even supply free party hats and paper horns for the celebration. I make some of my best tips on New Year's Eve as the official "soda jerk." That's what you call the person who works the soda fountain. That's not "jerk," as in "idiot." Although, sometimes I wonder.

Around ten o'clock, folks start returning from the Ruby Theater, where they're having a special New Year's showing of *King Kong,* the 1933 thriller which, I have already seen five times. I am in charge of making sure everyone has a party hat and a horn when they walk in our front door. By half past ten, Romeo and Juliet arrive on the scene. I stay right on their heels, ready to jump in at any minute, just in case they should get too chummy before midnight.

While I'm following them down the discount aisle, pretending to be re-arranging fly swatters, Billy Ray starts to put his arm around Emma Jean. *Good Golly Miss Molly* by Little Richard is playing on the radio, giving me a perfectly good reason to start dancing. I go twisting down the middle of the aisle swinging a fly swatter back 'n forth, keeping in step to the music and *accidentally* swat Emma Jean away from Billy. "Oh, Emma Jean, I am *so* sorry!" It seems a completely appropriate time to begin a conversation about bugs with her since I'm holding a fly swatter. "Hey, did you know there over two hundred species of moths in North America?"

Emma Jean looks at me a little bewildered. "Um... that's... nice, Mazie."

Billy steps around me, and back over to Emma's side. "Oh, Billy, hi... I didn't see you there. Well... Happy New Year's!"

"Hey Mazie!" Sammy calls me from the soda counter. "You're on the fountain, get over here!"

I look back at Emma Jean and Billy. "Come by my counter for a free root beer float just before midnight. We'll drink a toast to the New Year."

******

The next two hours are pure torture. I'm stuck behind my soda counter while Emma Jean and Billy Ray flaunt their childish crush in the aisles of *my* store. I send Maybeline out every five seconds to bring me a Romeo and Juliet report. She finally tells me I'm nuts and plops herself down at the counter and talks to my brother instead. Just to add to my agony, Jesse Deere shows up and orders three sodas in a row while hounding me for the rest of my shift. I finally send him off to go find Emma Jean and Billy Baxter and remind them that it's time to come collect on their free root beer floats.

Finally, at eleven fifty-five P.M., I get an order from Emma Jean for a root beer float. I take my own sweet time making it, knowing that time is of the essence here. After I slowly roll the ice cream around to get it into a perfectly round-shaped ball, I plop it into the glass. Three minutes to go. Next, I pull the root beer handle and fill the glass—while staring at the clock. The root beer fizzes up and nearly overflows. I wait for it to settle back down. With sixty seconds left to go, the countdown has begun; "sixty, fifty-nine, fifty-eight..."

There is a wonderful product on the market that just came out on our shelves. I believe it was invented for special occasions like tonight. It's the same stuff Uncle Tooty used on Nellie's quarters. Super quick drying glue. While everyone else is busy counting down with the clock, I pull out my tiny tube of *Super Gloo.* I insert a straw into the root beer float and strategically place a dab of the *Super Gloo* around the entire lip zone of the straw. With thirty seconds left to go on the clock, I slide the float over to Emma Jean.

"Thanks, Mazie." Emma Jean leans over and takes a sip.

"Ten, nine, eight…"

Billy Ray slides his arm around Emma Jean's shoulder and scoots closer.

"Three, two, one… " Horns blast, sirens sound, lights flash…

Just as Billy Ray's face closes in on Emma Jean, she turns toward him…with a straw sticking straight out from between her lips, poking him in the face.

"Ouuww—my eye!" Billy Ray winces.

Emma Jean blurts out something that sounds like his name through her straw. "Oh, Biwwy Way!"

Bingo. The kiss is off.

There is so much commotion that no even notices what happened to Emma Jean until all the noise dies down and people can finally hear her muttering through her straw.

"Whoa—look at Emma Jean," someone in the crowd comments.

Now everyone's looking at Emma Jean. Her face looks like a rutabaga with a sunburn, and she can't for the life of her pull that straw out of her mouth without pulling her lips right off with it. I am enjoying myself more than I have all night…'til I realize the *Super Gloo* tube is stuck fast to the palm of my hand from squeezing it so tight all this time. Now Emma Jean can't remove the straw and begins to cry… and I can't remove the evidence.

"Miss Mazie," Daddy says, "help me get this place cleared out, so we can start cleaning up."

"Yes, sir." *I'll be glad to. The sooner I can get Emma Jean out the door, the better my chances of not getting caught for the crime.*

Just as I'm thinking that, Emma Jean makes so much noise crying through that straw, Daddy looks over her way. "Emma Jean," he says, "what is up with that straw on your lips?"

Billy Ray is looking mighty worried. "Mr. Farley, something is on that straw that's stuck tight to her lips."

"Let me see that," Daddy says, and leans over the counter to check it out.

I quickly close my hand into a tight fist and hide it behind my back.

"You got yourself stuck pretty good there, don't you?"

"Mmm-hmm," Emma Jean moans.

Now I'm starting to sweat a little.

"Seems to me," Daddy says, "that straw somehow cemented itself to your lips. Did Mazie serve this to you?"

"Mmm-hmm." She nods.

I suddenly pull my hand out from behind my back. "Well, I'll be—would you look at that! This tube must have stuck itself right to my hand when I reached in that drawer—and then I grabbed that straw for you!"

Daddy looks down at my hand, then back at Emma Jean. "Well, I'll be," he mutters. "I can take some turpentine to Mazie's hand to remove the tube, but that's not a good idea where your lips are concerned. Let's see what I got in the back that might work."

I'm feeling a little queasy over the whole ordeal.

Daddy comes back with a few different things to try on Emma Jean's lips. Between all of his soaps and solutions, he finally works the straw off. Now her lips are bright red and looking mighty sore. The name "soda jerk" suddenly pops back into my head.

Daddy goes in the back room to find the turpentine to try and get this tube off of my hand. All of a sudden, Billy Ray takes Emma Jean's little face in his hands, and says, "I know I'm a few minutes late on this, but, Happy New Year's, Emma Jean," then he swoops right in and lays a gentle kiss right on her cheek.

Cheek? *Cheek!* I did all of this just to stop a peck on the *cheek?* Which, by the way, I didn't stop anyway. *Uggghhh!* I just can't win for losing in this town. I've lost the only man I've ever loved. My life is good as over. As they say in Romeo and Juliet, *"Oh, happy dagger."*

9

Dancing Lessons

On my way home from school, I stop in at the post office to check P.O. Box # 30. I'm sifting through the mail, while meandering toward the Five-and-Dime, when suddenly, my name pops up on big bright yellow envelope addressed to Miss Mazie May Farley. I plop myself right down on the sidewalk and rip it open. A picture of a ballerina dancer appears on the front. Opening the card, I instantly recognize in my Aunt Birdie's handwriting.

Our Dearest Mazie,

Your Grandma Blossom and I have been discussing your upcoming birthday. We realize it's not until the end of the month, but we decided to surprise you a little early this year. We know y'all wanted to take some dancing lessons so you could attend the Sweetheart

Dance on Valentine's Day. We thought it best if you could start a little sooner than your birthday so you'd have plenty of time to learn the waltz correctly before the dance comes along. We have signed you up to begin your first dance lesson at the grange starting this next Friday night. Here's to our little Miss Mazie May—the Belle of the Valentine Ball—Happy Birthday!

Bundles of Love from,

Grandma Blossom, Aunt Birdie, and Uncle Tooty

This must be a sign that it's really going to happen!

While I'm busy sweeping the discount aisle, Elvis Presley comes on the radio, singing *Love Me Tender*. My broom stick instantly transforms into Billy Ray Baxter. I close my eyes and sweep through the aisle, twirling and swirling with my dream boy broom. *Please, please, please, let Billy Ray be in my dancing class Friday night.*

Sammy cuts right into my magic moment. "Mazie, when you're done dancing with that broom, you need to clean the restroom."

Brothers have a way of pulling your head back out of the clouds, and fast.

******

Friday night, pretty near every junior high school kid in town shows up at the grange. Ballroom dancing is a very popular social activity in Hog Eye, mostly because for all of the parents it was the only thing there was to do in Hog Eye when they were growing up, and they obviously plan to keep the tradition going. Also, with Elvis coming on the scene, parents are afraid their kids might turn into hip-swiveling hoodlums. A good reason for them to instill some old timer's dance traditions into our young, impressionable souls while there is still hope. One look around the room and you can tell which kids want to be here, and which kids were dragged here by their parents. Most of the girls don't seem to mind much, but you can tell the majority of the boys would rather be out hunting rabbits or doing just about anything besides dancing with girls.

Our dance instructors are Mr. and Mrs. Swan, a husband and wife team, who have won about every dance competition in Kentucky. They start off by showing us what a true waltz is supposed to look like when done properly. They've got some pretty close bodily contact going on that is making the girls a little nervous, and the boys are looking like they're about to be sick.

******

"Alright, gentlemen," Mr. Swan, announces, "I'd like each of you young men to ask a young lady if you may have the next dance."

Nobody moves.

"If y'all don't ask someone right now, I will just start matching you up myself."

That got a few of the bold ones moving.

I'm looking around, hoping with all my heart that Billy Ray is somewhere among that huddle of boys.

"May I have this dance, Miss Mazie?"

My heart starts to pound nearly out of my chest. I swing around with the words "Yes you may, Billy Ray!" on the tip of my tongue, only to find myself eye to eye with Jesse Deere. "Oh… it's you."

Jesse is dressed in a white shirt with a black tie, actually looking surprisingly handsome for Jesse. His Mama must have dressed him tonight. He usually runs around in torn up jeans and flannel shirts with his dark hair tousled all over.

In the most ladylike voice I can muster, I quietly reply, "I'd rather dance with a skunk, thank you," and curtsy. Then I see Lance Malroy, The Five-and-Dime Stalker, standing right behind Jesse, with his squinty little eyes and crew cut. He's the guy who comes into the Five-and-Dime and hides in the paper products aisle and spies on me from between the paper towel rolls. I can always tell when he's there because his crew cut sticks straight up above the paper towel rolls.

I quickly change my mind. "But, since there aren't any skunks in here, I guess I'll settle for you."

"Hey, this isn't exactly my idea of fun, either," Jesse says. "My dad gave me the choice between cleaning out the entire chicken coop, or learning to dance."

"Gee, I feel honored—I guess that means I rank a step above a stinking chicken."

"And I rank a step below a stinking skunk. I'd say we make a perfect couple. Shall we dance?"

"Face your partner and hold them like this." Mr. Swan takes Mrs. Swan in a close frontal position. I have never seen so many red faces in one room before. I look around the dance floor at couple after couple who look like two positive magnets repelling each other. They have their hands as close as they can get without actually touching, like there's some invisible force keeping them apart.

Mr. Swan comes by and helps us all make the final contact. The music starts up and Mr. Swan moves on to the next step. Jesse suddenly grabs my hand tight and whisks me off into the middle of the dance floor.

"Let go of me!" I yell, but he just starts twirling me under his arm, faster and faster, like I'm Ginger Rodgers and he's Fred Astaire. He gets me spinning so fast that I trip, and we both end up on the floor in a tangled heap! We have disrupted the entire dance lesson and have the whole grange in fits of laughter. I'm laying here thinking how funny this would be if it were happening to someone besides me!

Mr. Swan yells, "You two smart Alec's, knock off the charades!" Like I had something to do with this.

By the time the place is back under control, everyone seems to have loosened up from laughing so hard.

"I think we did them all a great big favor," Jesse says.

"Speak for yourself," I mutter, under my breath.

"Mr. Deere and Miss Farley," Mr. Swan bellows across the dance floor, "since I *apparently* have to keep a closer eye on you two, let's bring y'all out here to be my demo-couple."

Oh, joy. *Jesse Deere, you will regret the day you ever met me.*

******

I leave my first dance lesson on probation. "One more disruption like tonight, and your parents will be notified," we're warned on our way out the door.

I glare at Jesse.

"Thanks for the dance," he says, with a bow, and runs off toward home.

All I can say is, *Billy Ray, you'd better be worth all this.* The things we do for love.

10

Discount Aisle Dreamer

Monday afternoon, I'm dusting the shelves in the discount aisle when Paul Anka comes on the radio singing *You Are my Destiny.* I'm floating along with my feather duster, dreaming about the day Billy Ray realizes that *I* am his destiny. I'm picturing him down on his knees, proposing to me, right here in the discount aisle, with a big honking diamond ring—with two rubies on each side. I even hear wedding bells. I suddenly realize it's the bells on the front door I'm hearing. They jingle me right out of my daydream. Then I hear Sammy. "Hey Billy Boy, 'bout time you stopped by."

I quickly move myself to the convenience foods aisle and stake out behind the cereal boxes. This way I can arrange the boxes any way I need to in order to spy a little better. I have my nose perched between the Banana Whacky's and Capt'n

Smacky's, in perfect view of Billy Ray. He's wearing my favorite flannel shirt too—the blue and green one.

"Yeah, been keeping pretty busy working weekends at the *Come-N-Get-It* feed store. They even have me in there on Friday nights."

So that explains why he's not at dancing lessons.

"Seeing much of Emma Jean?" Sammy asks. I cock my ear a little closer, but can barely hear what they're saying.

"Not lately with this schedule."

Ha! Pity. Imagine my disappointment.

Next, Billy Ray says, "So, you planning on asking anyone to the Sweetheart Dance?"

Sammy's shuffling his feet around, acting funny. "Maybe," he says.

"So, who is she?"

Yeah, Sammy, who is she? I'm dying to know myself. I had no idea Sammy was sweet on anyone.

"None of your beeswax, buddy,—at least 'til I get up the nerve to ask her first. I s'pose you're planning on asking Emma Jean?"

"There's only one thing that will keep me from taking Emma Jean to the dance."

"What's that?" Sammy asks.

This I have got to hear. *Perhaps… if Sammy's little sister would be willing to go with him instead.* I climb one shelf higher so I can see him better when he says my name. Just as he starts to tell him, I grab onto the top shelf for support, but lose my balance and end up taking the whole shelf down with me! I tumble to the floor, along with every cereal box on the shelf.

Sammy and Billy Ray come running over and find me buried beneath a ton of cereal. I'm picturing my epithet on my grave stone: "Here lies Mazie May Farley buried beneath Banana Wacky's and Capt'n Smacky's, all for the sake of love. May she rest in peace."

"Mazie, are you okay under there?" Billy Ray asks.

"How in the world did you get yourself in that mess?" Sammy adds.

"It's a long story," I mumble from beneath the rubble. "Can you just dig me outta here?" Now I will never know what Billy Ray was gonna say, and even if it was about me, I probably just botched the whole dang deal. Who would want to take a klutz like me to a dance, anyway?

11

Dancing Lesson Two

I show up late to class on purpose, hoping they've already paired people off. I seriously doubt Mr. Swan will let me and Jesse dance with each other again, but my other options may not be much better. Maybe I'll just get to watch from the sidelines.

No such luck. Mr. and Mrs. Swan are out fluttering around the room like two birds in synchronized flight. They waltz their way around the grange three or four times before coming to a graceful halt in the middle of the dance floor. I guess this is a demo of what we're *supposed* to shoot for.

"Alright gentlemen, time to choose your partner. To save on time, it might be a good idea to have the same partner that you had last week."

I quickly hide myself behind a group of girls huddled in the corner—maybe Jesse hasn't seen me yet. Hopefully, he'll just ask someone else.

"Hey, there, Mazie, whatcha doing over here in the corner?"

It's *yours truly*, Jesse Deere, in his white shirt and bright red bow tie.   "How in the Sam Hill did you spot me?"

"I saw you come through the front door, and followed you—just in case you needed rescuing from some weirdo wanting to dance with you."

"They don't come any weirder than you, Jesse."

"Feel free to take your chances, but it looks to me like everyone else is paired off—except Lance Malroy."

I see Lance standing behind Jesse, just waiting for me to turn Jesse down.

I give up. "Looks to me like I'm stuck with you again."

"Yep, I guess so." He just smiles, and leads me out on the dance floor. "Stuck like Super Gloo on a straw, you might say."

I pull him back with a jerk. "What? Who told you about that?"

Jesse turns to face me, smirking. "Nobody told me. I was there and saw the whole thing myself. Even saw you putting that glue right on that straw and serving it up to Emma Jean."

"You—you…"

"Don't you worry, Mazie Farley, your secret is safe with me—especially if you'll be my dance partner every week."

I nearly jerk his arm right out of the socket trying to pull my hand free, but he won't let go. "You—you can't force me to be your partner every week!"

"You're right." He drops my hand. "But then I can't guarantee that the town of Hog Eye won't find out how that glue got on Emma Jean's straw. I'm sure Billy Baxter would be mighty surprised to know."

"Are you trying to blackmail me, Jesse Deere? Because if you are, you'd be better off driving your John Deere tractor into a bale of hay than to mess with me, buddy."

Jesse looks at me with a calm, sweet smile that makes me want to whop him on the head. "Shall we dance?" he says, holding out his hand like he's a real gentleman.

I slam my hand back into his and drag my feet into the ready position. Once Billy Ray is mine, this will all be behind me.

12

Girl Talk

I'm sweeping up the soda shop floor, when someone comes clippity-clopping up to my broom and parks their pink fringed cowgirl boots right in front of me.

"Nellie!"

"Hey there, li'l padner, how are things with my best chow hound?"

"Not so good, if you really want to know."

Nellie takes a seat at my counter and pats the stool next to her for me to sit down. "Tell me what's eatin' ya, sugar."

I lean my broom against the wall, and take a seat facing her. "My life's a shambled mess," I confess.

"This sounds serious." Nellie fluffs her pink skirt out around the stool, then folds her hands in her lap like she's not going anywhere 'til I tell her everything that's wrong in my world.

"Nellie, have you ever found yourself stuck in the middle of a love triangle before?"

The corners of Nellie's mouth begin to twitch, but she takes a deep breath, then says, "Oh, this sounds a bit complicated. Can you tell me a little more?"

"Well, I happen to be in love with someone, who happens to be in love with someone else, and she happens to love him back, but he winks at me like maybe he secretly loves me, but I was too young for him when he fell in love with her, but now I'm not too young, so maybe he really loves me now, but just isn't sure how to dump the one who still loves him."

"Ah. That's quite a tangle you got yourself in there."

"Well, like the song goes, *"Love Is A Many Splintered Thing."*"

"I think that's *'Splendored Thing,'* you're thinking of." Nellie's mouth is twitching again. "But in your case, maybe 'splintered' is a better word." Nellie looks like she's thinking things over for a minute. "Hmm, I can't say I've been in your exact boots, but I do know how it feels to be in love with someone who may not know that you love them, and you don't know if they could, or would ever love you back."

"Oh, Nellie, how could anyone not love *you* back?"

"I wish I were that confident, but to tell you the truth, I'm kind of chicken to find out."

"Well, I think you need to let that person know you love them, or you might just die a lonely old lady, when you could have had a nice man to shell peas with out on your front porch."

"Hey, I'm barely thirty years old yet!"

"Nellie," I say, "time waits for no one. If you want a good man to spend the rest of your life with, you'd better let him know how you feel and nail him down now."

Nellie laughs, then smiles, then looks serious. "Hmm, you might just have a point there." She nods her head a few times. "As for you, little missy, does this fella of yours know you like him?"

"Love, Nellie. Not *like*. I *love* him.

"Well, first off, it's not a good thing to come in the middle of two people who have feelers for each other. But since nobody's married here, and you don't know his true feelers, maybe let him know in some small way that you care about him, then see how he responds. But you have to be willing to accept that he may not return your same feelers. The other thing is about believing in serendipity.

"What on earth is seren-whatever-you-called-it?"

"Serendipity. It's when life brings you a pleasant surprise. And it may not be exactly *what* you were hoping for, or even *when* you were hoping for it. It's a kinda outta the blue surprise. Sometimes serendipity is a good way to go when it comes to love. You know, like leaving things to fate."

"But we're talking *true love* here, Nellie. I don't want to leave *true love* to fate. What if you end up with a dorky serendipity?"

"Not possible."

"Why not?"

"Because, if serendipity means 'pleasant surprise,' you can't have a dorky surprise or it wouldn't be serendipity."

"Oh. But is there such thing as *true love serendipity?*"

"Sure there is."

"Then I want to get me one of those. A true love serendipity.

"Well, you can always hope for one. But one thing I do know for sure, you can't *make* someone love you. You just have to cast your bread out on the waters and see what happens. But, if love doesn't come back to you on its own, you have to be willing to let it float on down stream."

"Okay, Nellie, I'll make a deal with you. I'll toss my bread out there on the waters if you toss yours out too. Deal?"

Nellie looks around the store a bit, lets out a big sigh, then puts out her hand to shake on it. "Deal," she says.

As soon as we seal the deal, I look up and see Daddy heading over our way, so I reach over and grab my broom. I'm just waiting to hear, "Cut the chit-chat and get back to sweeping, Miss Mazie." Instead, Daddy just gets a big smile on his face. "Hey there, Miss Nellie, what a nice surprise to find you here."

Nellie stands up and says, "Hi there, Mr. Farley." She reaches up and puts her pretty blonde hair behind her ears.

"Please, call me Pete." Daddy says back.

Pete? Call me Pete? Nobody calls my Daddy Pete, 'cept his relatives—everyone else calls him Peter or Mr. Farley. I just shrug my shoulders and start sweeping.

"Mazie and I were just having a little girl talk here," Nellie tells him. "I'm sorry if I distracted her from work."

"Oh, not a problem at all, you feel free to come chat with Mazie anytime. We run a pretty loose ship around here."

Loose ship? Here? Is this really my Daddy talking? I turn around and look at the two of them. Nellie is shuffling her pink boots back and forth and twisting her hair in little knots, and Daddy's talking crazy. Grown-ups can act so strange at times.

13

Clean up on Aisle Three

I'm working the store alone with Sammy on Saturday morning while Daddy's out on deliveries. The minute Elvis comes on the radio singing *You Ain't Nothing But A Hound Dog,* me and Sammy each grab a broom and pretend to be playing guitars while doing our Elvis moves along with it. We're laughing our heads off, when, suddenly, I look out the front window and see Mrs. Sable coming down the walk with her big, shaggy English sheep dog, Ellsworth. *Oh great. Daddy's not even here to deal with her.* "Sammy, get ready, it's Mrs. Sable."

Sammy suddenly stops and throws down his broom. "She's all yours," he says, and heads for the back room. "I'm stocking shelves."

Just my luck.

Daddy raised me and Sammy on these five words; *"The customer is always right."* That has always been our store policy, which is one reason we get stuck with all the customers that nobody else wants shopping in their stores. They come to our store where they can blame everything that's wrong in their lives on us. Daddy says not to worry, when we all get to heaven it will all even out. I think Daddy is gonna have one big gold crown full of jewels for all the demands and insults he's taken from Mrs. Sable. I'm not so sure about me. I'll be lucky to get a paper crown.

We generally don't allow dogs in our store, but Mrs. Sable insists that Ellsworth is a seeing-eye dog. He has so much hair covering his eyes that he bumps into things constantly. But Mrs. Sable swears she can hardly see two inches in front of herself without him. That's also her excuse for handing us her shopping list every week and expecting us to run around and get everything for her—while

Ellsworth runs around bumping into things, and piddling on our floors in the dog food aisle.

"Morning Mrs. Sable," I say, in my pretend pleasant voice.

She looks around without answering. "Is your father in?"

"No, ma'am," he's on a delivery this morning."

"So it's just you, is it?"

"Yes, ma'am. Sammy's stocking shelves. Can I get something for you, Mrs. Sable?"

"No, you may not. As a matter of fact, the reason I'm here is to return something I bought that I'm not a'tall happy with."

While she's busy pulling something out from her bag, Ellsworth goes running off to the dog food aisle. I'm listening to things fall from the shelves and hit the floor as he makes his way through the store by Braille. The phrase 'blind leading the blind' comes to my mind.

Mrs. Sable plunks a pair of rain booties down on my counter and says, "These did not hold up well a'tall and already have holes in them. I'd like a new pair or a refund."

I'm staring at a pair of rubber booties that are full of teeth marks. "Why, Mrs. Sable, it looks to me like maybe Ellsworth got a hold of these and chewed them up."

Mrs. Sables nostrils begin to flare in and out. "Are you trying to accuse my Ellsworth, rather than take the responsibility of selling me a poor quality product?"

"No m'am, I'm just saying that since you can't see all that well, that maybe you couldn't see that these holes are made from dog teeth."

"How dare you insult my judgment, Miss Sassy Pants! I happen to have a receipt right here that says if I am not satisfied with the quality of a product, I may return it for a full refund." She slams the receipt down in front of me and taps the store policy with her long, pointy, bright red fingernail.

"Well then, Mrs. Sable, I'd say this is your lucky day, 'cause if you can see that receipt well enough to read those tiny words, then you must be healed from your blindness! Hey—now you can start shopping for yourself, and you won't be needing a seeing-eye dog anymore—in which case I'm sorry to say that non-working dogs are not allowed in our store, so Ellsworth will have to wait outside from now on and won't be allowed to come in here and knock everything off of our shelves and pee all over our floors anymore."

I have never seen anyone breathe fire before but if anyone ever could, this would be the lady to do it. "Why, you wicked girl, I have half a mind to get you fired, and don't think I won't."

"Well, Jimmy cracked corn, and I don't care! I'm pretty sick and tired myself of hearing *'clean up on aisle three'* every time you and your dumb dog come in our store!"

Mrs. Sable squints her beady little eyes at me from behind her cat-rimmed eye glasses with the fake diamonds. "You just wait until your Father hears about this…"

111

"I believe I just heard it all, Mrs. Sable."

I whip around and see my Daddy in the doorway of the back room. *I'm a dead duck.*

"Mazie May Farley, you apologize to Mrs. Sable right now."

"But Daddy, her dog comes in here and messes everything up and piddles, and I'm always the one who…"

"I said *now,* Mazie May." Daddy's using his deep down voice which means I'd better just say it."

"I'm sorry, Mrs. Sable."

"Miss Mazie, you go on up to The Loft. I'll help Mrs. Sable, then I'll be up to talk to you."

"Yes, sir." I make my way down aisle three and have to step over the canned food and Ellsworth's puddle, just to get to the back staircase. *Dumb dog.*

******

I'm sitting on the edge of my bed just waiting for Daddy to show up and fill me in on my punishment. *"You ain't nothin' but a hound dog"* is wafting up through the radiator from the store speakers. I wonder if Daddy really will fire me. He does not tolerate disrespect of any kind, especially toward the blind—or people claiming to be blind. I don't know what got into me. I'm thinking that maybe being caught up in this love triangle has finally made me snap.

I hear Daddy's footsteps coming up the back stairs. This is one day I may live to regret—if I live, that is. Daddy opens the door. He stares at me for a minute, then he covers his mouth with his hand and suddenly bursts out laughing. He's laughing so hard he has to bend over, holding himself up with his hands on his knees. He finally looks up at me. "Mazie, don't ever do that again, you hear me?" He shakes his head, turns around, and goes back downstairs.

What on earth has come over my daddy lately?

14

Dancing Lesson Three

I show up on time this week, resigned to the fact that Jesse is my partner. Low and behold, he is no where to be found. At first I'm relieved—until Lance Malroy appears in front of me. "Miss Mazie, would you be my partner tonight?"

Lance is wearing dark pants—six inches too short and six inches too wide—held up by suspenders. He looks just like a mole with his squinty eyes.

"Lance, don't you usually wear glasses?"

"Um… I did… until I stepped on them last week doing the tango. They're being repaired this week."

"Ah." At this point I'm actually praying for Jesse Deere to come walking through that door. "Well, I'm kinda waiting to see if Jesse is coming tonight since I'm supposed to be his partner."

Lance looks back toward the door and says, "I wouldn't count on it. The Deere's old coon dog has taken ill from what I hear. I don't expect to see Jesse here tonight."

"Well... maybe he'll show up late... I should probably wait and see."

"Not with ol' Dusty bein' sick, he won't. That dog's been Jesse's best friend nearly as long as he's been alive."

"How do you know all that?" I ask.

"The Deere's are my neighbors and my mama was talking to his mama about it. Says Jesse's mighty upset about it. Probably much too upset to dance."

Now I'm feeling pretty bad about that poor dog. I really do happen to love dogs, 'cept for Ellsworth, and he'd even be tolerable if he didn't make so much work for me.

Just as I'm about to resign myself to my new dance partner, a skinny little dark haired girl appears before us.

"Lance," she says, kinda quiet, "I believe we're supposed to have the same partner that we had last week." She looks down at her black patent leather Mary Jane's like that was the hardest thing she's ever had to say in her whole life.

I look at her then at Lance. Lance looks pretty surprised that someone is actually requesting him back. He suddenly gets a goofy grin on his face and says, "Why, gee, Miss Adeline, I didn't realize you were here."

I suddenly have a brilliant idea. "Hey, you two go ahead, I'm feeling real concerned about Jesse's dog, and I think I'd like to go check up on how he's getting on." With that, I turn and run out the big double doors!

I make my way down along Huckleberry Hollow 'til I get to the Deere's farm at the end of the road. It's pretty dark out, but the lights are burning bright out in the barn. Being that I can't see real good in the dark, the next thing I do is step right smack in the middle of a cow pie—in my good dancing shoes.

I go over to scrape my shoes off on the fence post and lean against the railing. Without much warning, that rail gives way and I splat right into the mud by the watering tank.

By the time I pull open the barn door I am a sight to behold. First thing I see is Jesse sitting in the hay with his dog lying at his side. He looks up and his eyes scan me over from head to toe. "If I didn't know better," he says, "I'd think you were Mazie Farley covered in mud."

"Well, like my daddy always says, 'if it looks like a duck and sounds like a duck... it probably is a duck'."

"Why aren't you dancing at the grange tonight?" Jesse asks.

"I decided to go dancing in your cow pasture instead, that's why." I slowly make my way over by Jesse and sit in the hay next to him. I figure all that hay is gonna stick right to the mud on my dress and I'm gonna look just like a scarecrow by the time I leave. "I heard your dog has taken sick and thought I'd come see how he's doing."

"Dusty ain't doing real good," he says. Vet thinks he might of ate something that didn't sit right, and says we'll just have to wait and see if it passes on through."

Dusty Deere. Funny what folks decide to name their dogs. Dusty looks like he's seen better days. His head is as limp as a wet noodle on Jesse's lap. I have never seen Jesse look so sad. I reach over and stroke Dusty's soft brown coat real gentle. Dusty looks at me and breathes a heavy sigh.

"I don't know what I'll do if I lose him," Jesse says, looking like he's about to cry.

I just sit beside Jesse, petting Dusty for a long time. I know how it feels to watch someone or something you love suffer. I watched Mama get real sick and I couldn't do a thing to help her. And I still don't know what to do now that she's gone. But the longer I sit here, the more I feel like I might just start to cry myself. I decide I'd better leave before that happens. "Well, Jesse, 'guess I'd better go now, before all this mud dries so hard I can't walk myself home. But I'm gonna pray for Dusty my whole way back home."

"Thanks, Mazie. You okay walking home alone? You can borrow my horse if you like."

That makes me laugh. "And do what—tie him to the front door of the store 'til morning?"

"Ol' Tex would just turn around and run back home if you told him to—horses always know their way home."

"Thanks, Jesse, but I'll be fine. It's not that far. Besides, I know every neighbor along the way back home." I get up and head toward the barn door, then turn around. Jesse has laid his own head down on the straw right next to Dusty's. I have an inkling he'll be spending the night right there.

******

Come morning, I see Jesse first thing at school and ask him how Dusty's doing. Jesse gets a big grin on his face. "Dusty passed a big rock this morning. He has a bad habit of fetching rocks. Guess he swallowed one that didn't sit right—but looks as though he's gonna pull through."

"That's good," I tell Jesse. A dog can sure Mean a lot to a kid.

15

Birthday Boots and Bandits

I am finally eligible to be Billy Ray Baxter's new girlfriend. I am officially twelve years old today. Just to make sure Billy Ray is aware of this fact, I'm throwing myself a birthday party at school in the lunchroom cafeteria. I made enough cupcakes for the first twenty-four people who come up and wish me a happy birthday. I made sure Sammy passed the word to his friends too. Our school goes all the way from kindergarten through high school, but I didn't tell any of the kids younger than eleven, or older than thirteen, about my birthday treats, just to improve the odds of Billy Ray getting in on the cupcakes. Once he realizes I am only one year younger than he is, it's adios, Emma Jean!

By lunch time, I have a whole trail of kids following me to the cafeteria. I set up my cupcakes right in the middle of my lunch table and yell,

"Come-n-get-'em!" I figure that alone will get Billy Ray's attention since it's like the name of the feed store he works at.

"Happy birthday, Mazie!" is all I hear, over and over and over.

By the time I'm down to my last few cupcakes, I start to get a little concerned that Billy Ray has not come collecting his yet. Just as some kid starts to grab my last cupcake, I snatch it right out from under him. "Sorry, pal, this one is reserved."

Just then, someone comes sweeping in front of me, wearing a black bandit mask like The Lone Ranger, swipes the cupcake right out of my hand and replaces it with a little wrapped gift package— wrapped in black. *Who... what?* I stand here just baffled as all get out. I didn't even get a chance to get a good look but he seemed about the size of Billy Ray.

I grab Maybeline and drag her out to recess, to a secluded corner on the playground. We both stare intently as I slowly open the package with extreme caution—just in case it's a trick, like last time Jesse Deere gave me a snake for Christmas. I gently lift the lid to the box and peek inside. Sitting on a layer of black tissue paper is the most adorable crystal mouse with a little silver head and tail. "Oh, look."

"It's just precious," Maybeline whispers. "Who do you s'pose it's from?"

I know exactly who it's from. "Billy Ray Baxter," I whisper back.

"*Billy?* Why do think it's Billy.

"It's obvious. Don't you get it?"

"Get what?"

"Maybeline, sometimes you are slower than molasses running uphill in a snow storm. It's wrapped in black."

"*So…*"

"*So*, it's our secret wrapping paper color—I told him it's the new romance color. It's a secret clue. Billy Ray can't let anyone know he likes me just yet. He has to find a nice way to dump Emma Jean before he publicly declares his love for me—so he had to disguise himself. Get it?"

"What makes you think it's not just Jesse Deere—he did give you a Christmas present, remember—that snake prank that scared the wits outta you?"

"That's how I know it's not Jesse. Unless this mouse blows up in the next five seconds, I'll know it's not from Jesse Deere."

I spend the rest of the day just wandering around in a dazed, crazed love stage. My life is finally coming together at age twelve. It can only go uphill from here. All I have to do now is let Billy Ray know that I have mutual feelers for him too.

******

For my family celebration, Daddy takes me and Sammy out to Country Vittles for a birthday dinner and dessert. Soon as we wolf down our three meatloaf specials, Nellie comes back with the dessert menus. Sammy goes and spills the beans about it being my birthday.

"Woo-hoo!" Nellie whoops so loud, the entire place hears her. "Mazie Farley, don't you move a muscle 'til I come back." Nellie swings her way back to the kitchen, looking stylish as ever in her red and white fringed shirt, a matching skirt and vest, and red cowgirl boots. Nellie must spend all her tips on her fancy boot collection. I can hardly wait 'til I can do that myself.

"Daddy," I say, "I think Nellie is the most beautiful waitress in the whole town, don't you?"

When I turn to look at Daddy, I can see he's watching Nellie swing her way back to the kitchen too. Without taking his eyes off of her, he says, "I think you may be right about that, Mazie."

"Yeah. It's too bad you're so old."

Daddy looks at me. *"So old?* Mazie, I'm only thirty-five."

"That's what I'm talking about. Too old for someone like Nellie. That's five years older than her—which is really too bad, 'cause Nellie says she'd really like to find a nice man she can nail down to shell peas with."

"Is that so?" Daddy says. He turns his head back toward the kitchen. Out comes Nellie sporting a big huge piece of cake piled a mile high with ice cream, and a candle flaming away on top.

"Happy Birthday, Miss Mazie," she says, and plops it right down in front of me. Then, before I have a chance to crawl under the table, Nellie whistles with a two-finger whistle and has the entire place singing happy birthday to me. After I'm redder than a boiled lobster, Nellie squats down beside me. "Hey li'l cowpoke, how 'bout if you and me go shopping for your birthday tomorrow for a nice pair o' cowgirl boots?"

"Really? I squeal. "Any color I want?"

"Any color you want—I mean, as long as it's okay with your daddy, that is."

I turn toward Daddy. "Is it, Daddy?"

"As long as they're comfortable enough to work in, and the heel's not too high." He smiles over at

Nellie. "Can't have her falling off her heels and hurting herself on the job."

"Gotcha." Nellie smiles back.

I am more excited than a mouse locked inside a cheese factory for a night!

******

Once we are all overdosed on *Country Vittle's* famous chocolate cake, with ice cream, Nellie swings back by our table. "Y'all ready for seconds?"

"Nooo," we all three moan.

"Well, alrighty then, but promise you'll come back in two weeks on my birthday and we'll do it again."

"Your birthday? What day?" I ask.

"Friday, the fourteenth of February."

"You're a Valentine baby! Wait… that's the night of the Sweetheart Dance—I'll be busy, but Daddy will come back—won't you Daddy?"

Daddy looks at Nellie and smiles. "Promise," he says.

"Good." Nellie smiles back.

Daddy thanks Nellie for making my birthday dinner so special.

Nellie says, "You're very welcome, Pete." Then she gives me a birthday hug and says, "I'll come by your store after school tomorrow and we'll head on over to The Boot Barn, okey dokey?

"Okey dokey," I say.

"Don't forget to make a wish on a star on your way home—birthday wishes almost always come true." She tears off our guest check, hands it to Daddy, and swings away.

Daddy leaves another big tip—probably to help cover my birthday boots.

******

On the walk home, I look up and make my wish on the brightest star I can find. I wish for serendipities all around—one for me, Sammy, Daddy, and Nellie. Between the secret birthday mouse, my birthday dinner, and my date for boot shopping, this has been the best birthday ever—especially because there is a birthday bandit out there who is secretly in love with me. And I have an inkling who it might be.

16

My Achy Breaky Heart

I have been racking my brain for some way to let Billy Ray know that I have feelers for him—without being *too* obvious. I've decided to write him an obscure love poem that he'll have to figure out to get the true message. I plan to secretly slip it into his locker at school.

Dear Billy,
I tossed my bread upon the water
Among the lovely little tadpoles
Frolicking amidst the swamp foliage
Hoping my crumbs will come back to me
Instead of getting eaten by the tad poles
My destiny is in the hands of the one who finds my crumbs
If my crumbs return then I'll know it was meant to be, you and me,

And I will share my crumbs with thee from now until eternity.

Love, forever & a day,

Your secret admirer

Hint: One of your best friend's little sisters who just turned 12.

As soon as I slip the poem under his lunch box on his locker shelf, Maybeline comes running up to me and grabs my arm. "Mazie, guess who's going to the Sweetheart Dance?"

I hope it's me. "Who?" I ask.

"Me!"

"You? *With who?*"

Maybeline cups her hand around her mouth, and whispers in my ear. *"Sammy!?"* I yell, completely in shock.

Maybeline cups her hand over my mouth. "Shhh!"

"Well, I'll be." *Will wonders never cease?* To think this whole time my brother has liked my best friend after all. *Maybe we can double date if all goes according to plan.*

******

Nellie walks me into the Boot Barn and within minutes has every salesperson in the place bringing out boots for me to try on. I love the pink ones like Nellie's, but the heels are too high. I love the red ones, but the sides are too tight. I love the black ones with the silver toes, but they're too stiff to walk in. After trying on black, green, red, blue, and pink in every style, I finally find a pair that's the perfect style, size, fit, and color. Nellie even has one of the salesmen put special silver taps on the bottom so they'll clip-clop when I walk—just like hers do.

While we're sitting, waiting for the tap man to do his work, Nellie starts fiddling with my hair. "You ever wear your hair in braids?" She asks.

"Used to," I say.

"Mind if I give it a go while we're waiting?"

"No."

Nellie digs through her big leather purse and pulls out a brush, a comb, a few rubber bands, and some pretty silver hair clips. She must have half a beauty parlor inside that purse of hers. "Hold these," she says, and stands behind my chair like we are just setting up shop right here.

Nellie takes her brush to my hair and brushes it out 'til all the kinks are gone. Then she just keeps brushing it over and over 'til it's smooth as silk. I forgot just how good it feels to have someone brushing my hair. I just close my eyes and remember how it used to feel. Don't think nobody's brushed it, but me, since Mama was here.

It makes my scalp tingle when Nellie parts my hair down the back with the tail of her rat tail comb. She weaves each side into a braid, then joins them together in back. When she's all done with the braiding, she pops a silver clip on each side, and comes around front to check her work. "Perfect," she says. Then, like magic, she whips a hand mirror out from her purse, and holds it in front of me.

I see someone staring back at me who I barely recognize. "Wow," I whisper. I don't want to appear conceited or nothing, but I can't stop staring at myself. For the first time in a real long time, I feel kinda pretty.

After hugging Nellie good bye at the corner, I clip-clop my way back into the Five-and-Dime, sporting my new bright blue cowgirl boots with fringe down the sides. Talk about happy feet! I go square dancing solo down the aisle and twirl my way behind the soda counter, never taking my eyes off my boots. When I look up… there's Billy Ray sitting right in front of me on one of our stools. "New boots?" he says.

My eyes nearly pop clear outta my head. Besides catching me dancing, I remember he must have read my poem. Dang, dang, double dang! He's probably here with a Marshall's order telling me not to come within fifty feet of him or his locker ever again. On the outside, I try to appear cool as a watermelon on ice. Inside, I'm a mess. "Hey, Billy, what can I get for you?" It's hopeless—my voice is shaking all over the place.

"Nothing actually. I'm just sitting here waiting to talk to you."

"No Marshall orders...warrant for my arrest... nothing like that?"

"Um... no, nothing like that." He gives me a funny smile. "Oh, hey, thanks for the poem, by the way. That was from you, wasn't it?"

He read it. How embarrassing. "So—so, did you hate it, or what?"

"No, I didn't hate it at all. That's why I wanted to talk to you." He looks around, then says real quiet, "I have something I want to ask you."

I freeze. *My crumbs are coming back.* Now that this moment has finally come I can't believe it. He's really gonna ask me to the Sweetheart Dance. I just stare at him, afraid to move a muscle for fear he'll change his mind.

"Well, I..."

"Hey, Mazie! Where do y'all keep your rawhide dog bones?" someone yells from aisle one.

Dog bones? At a time like this? I know that voice. I am so irked at Jesse Deere right now I could spit nails. "Look for yourself," I yell back, in a not so nice voice. "Try the *dog* aisle." I don't have time to worry about Jesse Deere's dumb dog bones right now. I have to get back to Billy Ray asking me to that dance before he forgets what he came here for. "Now what was it that you wanted to ask me?"

He scoots around on the stool, and starts over. "Well... you know that Sweetheart Dance that's coming up?"

I nod. *Breathe,* I remind myself.

I was wondering, Mazie, if... you... uh..."

I nod my head a little harder just to help encourage him along.

"If I were to buy a corsage... what color do you like best?"

Oh, a corsage! He's buying me a corsage. I can't think straight. "Umm, I guess... " I quickly look out the window for ideas. I'm staring at Lavender Lake. "My favorite color for a corsage would be... lavender." *Lavender! Why did I say Lavender? I hate lavender.* Billy Ray cocks his head to the side. "Lavender, huh?"

"Yeah, but any color would be fine if you picked it out," I say.

"No, I think lavender would be a real nice color." He grins at me with that adoring dimpled smile of his. "Thanks, Mazie. You've saved the day. I think Emma Jean will be real pleased with lavender. I figured from your taste in bugs, wrapping paper, and poetry, that you understand these things about girls that guys are pretty much clueless about."

"B-but... my poem... what about my poem?"

"That's what I mean, Mazie. Being a guy, I didn't really understand what your poem meant—about the bread and all, but I figured it was written by someone who understands all this girl stuff. That's why I'm so glad I have someone like you to go to for the girly-girl advice." Then he gets up, winks at me, and walks away.

But... but...

"Hey, Mazie?"

Still in a state of shock, I shift my eyes toward aisle and zero in on Jesse.

"Do you think Dusty would like a rawhide bone, or a ham hock from the butcher best?"

"Heck if I know! Why do guys always have to ask me what their girlfriends and dogs would like? Are y'all too dumb to think for yourselves? *Geez!"*

I leave Jesse standing there in the aisle holding a rawhide bone.

"I quit!" I yell, and clip-clop out the front door.

17

Blue Moon

There is a full moon filling the sky, lighting a path to the beach for me. I figure Lavender Lake is as good a place as any to try and sort out my sorry little life. After sitting on the dock a good long time, I hear footsteps behind me. When I turn around, Jesse's standing there. He's looking like he's afraid to take another step closer—probably thinking I'm gonna bite his head off if he does. I suddenly feel like a real creep.

"Hey, Jesse," I say, minus the witch-tone this time.

"Okay to join ya?" he asks.

I scoot over so he knows it's okay to come near me. He smells like ham, then I see he's carrying a little butcher bag. "So, you decided on the ham hock, huh?"

"Yeah. I just asked myself what I'd want if I were a dog, and ham sounded pretty good." He takes a seat next to me, and starts swinging his feet back and forth above the water.

I look Jesse right in the eye. "Jesse, I am very sorry for being such a jerk back there in the store."

He shrugs. "That's okay. Did Billy Ray say something to upset ya?"

"Naw. It's what he didn't say that upset me."

He just nods.

There is no way I'm gonna admit to Jesse that I was hoping to get asked to that dance by someone who just smashed my heart to smithereens and never even knew it.

Me and Jesse just sit here swinging our feet back and forth, watching our reflection in the water. "Hey, Jesse?"

"Yeah?"

"I'm real glad your dog is better."

He looks over at me and smiles. "Thanks, Mazie, me too."

We both look back down at the water.

"Hey, Mazie?"

"Yeah?"

"Your hair looks nice."

I'm glad he can't see me blush in my reflection from Lavender Lake.

******

The night of the Sweetheart Dance finally arrives, and I am not there. No, I have scheduled myself to run the store and am determined to set my mind on more important things than dumb dances and heartbreaking boys. As a consolation prize, God has granted me another full moon in the sky—that makes two in one month. A Blue Moon.

It's dead quiet in the store tonight. For the first time in ages Daddy has taken the night off— says he's popping over to *Country Vittles* to keep his promise to Nellie. I told him to go ahead 'cause I can run this place by myself 'til Sammy comes home from the dance. I sent Daddy off with a gift for Nellie—a set of little silver spurs earrings I bought

145

for her at Tina's Treasure Trough, and had 'em gift wrapped all fancy. Looked to me like Daddy was carrying a little gift of his own when he walked out the door.

******

I turn on my favorite country radio station to some boot stomping music, and get to work. After I sweep every aisle spotlessly clean, I start in on my soda counter, and begin dreaming about the day I get to have my own place. To make up for my deprived childhood, I plan to have a farm with ten dogs and five ponies, and grow sweet peas in bright pots. I never got to have a dog or a pony, or even a garden of my own before. I will just live my life with my flowers and my animals and die a single, solitary old woman. But I'll be happy. So happy... For some dumb reason, at this point in my daydream, I begin to sob.

I'm shining up my soda counter real good with a mix of bleach water and tears. The light of the moon is reflecting off the water across the way and lures me out to the side patio where I lean up against a lamp post with a deep sigh. My music is up so loud, I don't even hear the door jingle when someone comes out of the store behind me.

"Hey there, Mazie," someone says real kindly.

I turn around and find myself face to face with Jesse Deere. I quickly wipe my eyes, hoping it's dark enough out that he can't tell that I've been crying. "Hey, yourself, Jesse." He looks different tonight. All scrubbed up and wearing a new blue and green flannel shirt. "Ain't you going to the Sweetheart Dance?" I ask him.

"Nope," he says back, matter a fact.

"Why not?" I ask.

"Well," he says, looking at the moon, and then back at me, "the only girl I'd ever want to dance with ain't going."

"Funny," I say, surprised. "I thought I was the only girl in town not going to the dance."

He looks at me with that cocky smile of his, not saying a word.

I just stare right back into those deep brown eyes of his—which, I have never even noticed until right this very minute out here under these stars.

My favorite song, *Blue Moon of Kentucky,* comes on the radio.

"Hey Mazie… I know this is kind of a funny place to ask you this, but . . . may I have this dance?"

I suddenly feel a smile coming on. "… You may."

We face each other in the ready position, and start to laugh because *Blue Moon of Kentucky* is not exactly a ballroom dance song.

Then, with that bright Kentucky moon shining down on us, me and Jesse Deere waltz beneath the blue moon right on the patio of the Five-and-Dime.

******

There are times in life when everything once hoped for seems suddenly hopeless, and life begins to lose its shine. Then out of the blue, serendipity shows up and knocks your socks right off. I guess you could say this was one of those times. And we waltzed.

The End

From the memoirs of Mazie May Deere

About The Author

Renee Riva has been writing humorous, family and animal stories ever since she won her first writing contest in the second grade. A former greeting-card verse writer and popular speaker, Renee has also published three children's books: Izzy the Lizzy, Guido's Gondola, and Rudy the Runt, as well as a Young Adult trilogy: Saving Sailor, Taking Tuscany, and Heading Home. Farley's Five and Dime is her latest project about a fun and feisty little character named Mazie Farley.

Renee and her husband reside in Washington State with their three daughters, a dog, a cat, and a baby box turtle named Buster.

Find more exciting titles at:
www.thestonepublishinghouse.com and
www.reneeriva.com

STONEHOUSE INK